We hope this book has been informative and helpful on your journey to understanding and celebrating older adults. Thank you for your interest and support!

Title: Language and Technology-Exploring the Intersection of English, Blockchain, and AI
Subtitle: The Intersection of Innovation and Communication

Series: The Grammar Bible: Mastering the Rules and Conventions of English
By P. C. Dictionaire

"The English language is the sea which receives tributaries from every region under heaven."
Henry David Thoreau

"The English language is like a broad river on whose bank a few graceful trees are reflected, it is the language of a people who have a great past and who will have a great future."
Joseph Conrad

"The English language is the key to the world."
Neil Gaiman

"The English language is nobody's special property. It is the property of the imagination: it is the property of the language itself."
Derek Walcott

"The English language is the most important language in the world. It's the language of international business, politics, and entertainment."
Richard Branson

"The English language is a river that moves, and sometimes it flows backwards."
Alice Oswald

"The English language is a work in progress. Have fun with it."
Jonathan Culver

Table of Contents

The role of English language in technology and its evolution

English language has played a significant role in technology, and its evolution is something that is worth exploring. In this book, we delve into the intersection of English language, blockchain, and artificial intelligence. Before we dive into the details of this subject, let us first discuss the role of the English language in technology and its evolution.

The English language has been a prominent player in the field of technology. It is the most widely used language in the world and has become the lingua franca of the tech industry. English is the language of instruction and communication in universities, research institutions, and tech companies worldwide. The dominance of the English language in the tech industry can be attributed to historical, economic, and cultural factors.

The evolution of the English language in technology has been shaped by various factors. One significant factor is globalization, which has led to an increase in the use of English as a means of communication in the tech industry. The development of the internet and social media has also played a significant role in the evolution of English in technology. With the rise of digital communication platforms, English has become more informal, and new words and expressions have emerged.

Another factor that has shaped the evolution of the English language in technology is the influence of other languages. As technology becomes more global, the need to communicate in multiple languages has become more important. This has led to the emergence of hybrid languages, such as Chinglish, which is a mixture of English and Chinese.

The role of the English language in technology is not limited to communication. It also plays a significant role in the development of new technologies. Most of the programming languages used in the tech industry are written in English. Therefore, English proficiency is an essential skill for programmers and developers. The English language has also influenced the design of technology products, from user interfaces to product names.

As we explore the intersection of English language, blockchain, and artificial intelligence, we must consider the role that the English language has played in the development of these technologies. English is the language used in the development of blockchain and artificial intelligence, and proficiency in English is essential for individuals working in these fields.

In conclusion, the English language has played a significant role in the evolution of technology. As technology continues to develop, the role of the English language will only become more important. Understanding the intersection of English language, blockchain, and artificial intelligence is essential for anyone interested in the future of technology and its impact on our world.

Overview of the convergence of English, blockchain, and AI

The convergence of English language, blockchain, and artificial intelligence (AI) has brought about a new era of innovation and communication. In this introduction, we will provide an overview of this convergence and its significance in shaping the future of technology and language.

English language has always been the dominant language of technology and business. As technology continues to advance, English has become even more important as the language of global communication. This is because English is widely spoken and understood across the world. As a result, the ability to communicate in English has become an essential skill for individuals and businesses alike.

Blockchain technology, on the other hand, is a decentralized and secure method of storing and transferring data. It has become increasingly important in the digital age as it allows for secure transactions without the need for intermediaries. Blockchain technology is being used in various industries, such as finance, healthcare, and supply chain management.

Artificial intelligence, or AI, is the simulation of human intelligence processes by machines, especially computer systems. AI has the potential to revolutionize the way we live and work, from self-driving cars to intelligent personal assistants. The ability of AI to understand and process human language has also led to the development of natural language processing (NLP) technology, which enables machines to understand and interpret human language.

The convergence of English language, blockchain, and AI is significant because it enables the creation of new technologies that are not possible with just one of these elements alone. For example, the use of blockchain technology with English language could enable secure and decentralized communication across the world. Similarly, the use of AI with English language could lead to the development of intelligent language assistants that can help individuals communicate more effectively in a globalized world.

In this book, we will explore the intersection of English language, blockchain, and AI, and how this convergence is shaping the future of technology and communication. We will discuss the implications of this convergence for individuals, businesses, and society as a whole. We will also examine the challenges and opportunities presented by this convergence, and how we

can navigate them to create a more connected and innovative
world.

Purpose and scope of the book

English, blockchain, and AI are all innovative technologies that have the potential to revolutionize the way we communicate and interact with each other. The convergence of these three fields has created a new and exciting intersection, one that offers endless possibilities for the future of language and technology.

The purpose of this book is to explore this intersection in-depth and examine the ways in which English, blockchain, and AI are influencing each other. We will delve into the current state of the technology and explore how it has evolved over time, as well as speculate on the future of this convergence.

The scope of this book is broad, as it covers a range of topics related to the intersection of English, blockchain, and AI. We will explore how these technologies are being used to develop new applications and tools, and examine the implications of this convergence for the way we communicate and interact with each other. We will also discuss the challenges and opportunities that arise from this intersection, such as the potential for increased automation and the need to balance innovation with ethical considerations.

Through this book, readers will gain a deeper understanding of the role that English language plays in technology, and how it is being shaped by the convergence of blockchain and AI. It is our hope that this exploration of the intersection of language and technology will inspire readers to think critically about the future of communication and innovation, and the potential impact that these technologies may have on our lives.

Chapter 1: English Language in the Age of Blockchain and AI

The current state of the English language

The English language has become the most widely used language in the world, due in large part to the rise of globalization and technology. As such, it has taken on a significant role in the development of blockchain and AI. The current state of the English language is constantly evolving, and it is important to understand the changes that are taking place in order to stay up to date with the latest developments.

One of the biggest changes that the English language is experiencing in the age of blockchain and AI is the rise of new terminology. With the development of new technologies comes the need for new words to describe them. For example, terms such as "smart contract," "tokenization," and "decentralized" have become commonplace in the blockchain space, while terms like "machine learning," "neural network," and "natural language processing" have become central to the field of AI.

Another key aspect of the current state of the English language in the age of blockchain and AI is the increasing importance of technical writing skills. As more and more people enter the tech industry, it is becoming essential to be able to communicate complex technical ideas in a clear and concise manner. This has led to a renewed focus on technical writing skills in universities and technical schools, as well as in the workplace.

Additionally, the use of English in the development of blockchain and AI has also led to a rise in the importance of cross-cultural communication. With people from all over the world working together to develop new technologies, it is essential to be able to communicate effectively across cultural and linguistic barriers. As such, English has become the de facto language of international business and technology, and proficiency in English is becoming increasingly important for professionals in these fields.

Overall, the current state of the English language in the age of blockchain and AI is characterized by rapid change and increasing importance. It is essential for anyone working in these fields to stay up to date with the latest developments in the language in order to communicate effectively and stay ahead of the curve.

The role of blockchain and AI in language development

As the world becomes more interconnected, technology has played a significant role in shaping the English language. In recent years, blockchain and artificial intelligence (AI) have emerged as two of the most influential technological advancements that are transforming the way we communicate and interact with language. In this chapter, we will explore the role of blockchain and AI in the development and evolution of the English language.

Blockchain technology, a decentralized system of recording information, has gained significant attention for its potential to revolutionize various industries, including finance, healthcare, and supply chain management. However, its impact on language development has been less explored. Blockchain can facilitate the creation of decentralized, peer-to-peer communication networks that bypass traditional intermediaries such as governments and corporations. This means that people from different parts of the world can communicate with each other directly, without relying on a centralized authority or language service provider. As a result, the language used in these networks may evolve organically and reflect the diverse linguistic backgrounds of its users.

Similarly, AI has the potential to revolutionize language development by improving language processing and generation capabilities. With the advancement of natural language processing (NLP) technology, machines can now understand, interpret, and generate language more accurately and efficiently than ever before. This has significant implications for language learning, translation, and communication. For instance, AI-powered language learning tools can personalize language instruction based on a learner's proficiency and learning style. AI-powered translation tools can improve the accuracy and speed of translation, enabling seamless communication across different languages and cultures.

However, the role of blockchain and AI in language development is not without its challenges. While blockchain technology has the potential to promote linguistic diversity, it can also lead to the fragmentation of language and the emergence of new dialects that may be difficult to understand for speakers of other dialects. Additionally, the use of AI-powered language tools raises concerns about the accuracy and cultural appropriateness of machine-generated language.

Overall, the role of blockchain and AI in language development is complex and multifaceted. In this chapter, we will delve deeper into the ways in which these technologies are shaping the English language and explore the challenges and opportunities they present for language development in the age of blockchain and AI.

Challenges and opportunities for English in the era of blockchain and AI

As blockchain and AI technologies continue to advance, they present both challenges and opportunities for the English language. In this chapter, we will explore the potential impact of these technologies on the future of English.

One of the primary challenges that English faces in the era of blockchain and AI is the possibility of homogenization. As English becomes the lingua franca of technology and global commerce, there is a risk that other languages and dialects will be marginalized or even disappear. This could lead to a loss of linguistic diversity and cultural heritage.

However, blockchain and AI also offer unique opportunities for English language development. For example, AI language models such as GPT-3 have already revolutionized natural language processing and can facilitate communication across different languages. Blockchain technology can also facilitate language learning and language translation through decentralized platforms that incentivize users to contribute to language-related projects.

Another challenge for English is the need for constant evolution and adaptation in response to new technologies and emerging trends. As blockchain and AI continue to evolve, the English language must also adapt and develop new vocabulary and concepts to keep pace with the changing landscape.

In this chapter, we will also discuss the potential ethical and social implications of the convergence of English, blockchain, and AI. For example, the rise of AI language models raises questions about who controls language development and what biases may be present in the algorithms that power these models.

Overall, this chapter will explore the complex relationship between English, blockchain, and AI, and the challenges and opportunities that lie ahead for the future of the English language.

Implications for the future of the language

As blockchain and AI technologies continue to advance, their impact on the English language is becoming increasingly clear. The potential for these technologies to transform the way we communicate and interact with one another is significant, and the English language will undoubtedly play a crucial role in this evolution.

One key implication of blockchain and AI for the English language is the potential for increased standardization and homogenization. With blockchain enabling greater transparency and accountability in global communication, and AI facilitating greater automation and efficiency, there is a growing need for a universal language that can be understood and utilized across borders and industries. This may lead to a reduction in linguistic diversity and variation, as well as an increased emphasis on standardized forms of English.

At the same time, however, blockchain and AI may also create opportunities for new forms of linguistic expression and creativity. For example, blockchain technology could enable new forms of decentralized communication and collaboration that allow individuals to freely experiment with and develop new modes of expression. Similarly, AI may enable new forms of language processing and understanding that can facilitate more natural and nuanced communication between humans and machines.

Overall, the impact of blockchain and AI on the English language is likely to be complex and multifaceted. While these technologies may pose challenges to linguistic diversity and creativity, they may also create new opportunities for innovation and growth. As we move into an increasingly connected and technology-driven world, it will be important to continue monitoring and exploring the evolving role of English in this rapidly changing landscape.

Chapter 2: Blockchain Technology and its Impact on Language

Overview of blockchain technology and its applications

In recent years, blockchain technology has emerged as a game-changing innovation with the potential to transform various sectors, including finance, healthcare, and supply chain management. At its core, a blockchain is a decentralized, distributed digital ledger that records transactions in a secure, transparent, and tamper-proof manner. The technology enables participants to verify and authenticate transactions without the need for intermediaries, such as banks or government agencies.

The first and most well-known application of blockchain technology is cryptocurrency, such as Bitcoin and Ethereum. However, the technology has since expanded into other areas, including smart contracts, identity verification, and digital asset management. The use cases for blockchain are constantly expanding, and it is expected to become more prevalent in various industries in the years to come.

One of the most significant impacts of blockchain technology is its potential to revolutionize the way we communicate and interact with one another. Blockchain's decentralized nature allows for greater transparency and security in communication, making it an attractive option for businesses and individuals alike. It also has the potential to eliminate language barriers and promote cross-cultural communication, as information can be shared and verified in real-time without the need for translation.

Overall, blockchain technology has the potential to revolutionize the way we communicate and interact with one another. As the technology continues to evolve and expand into new areas, it will be interesting to see how it impacts language and communication in the years to come.

Use cases for blockchain in language-related fields

Blockchain technology is known for its unique ability to provide secure and transparent transactions without the need for intermediaries. These qualities make blockchain a valuable technology for various industries, including language-related fields.

One of the most promising use cases for blockchain technology in language-related fields is in the area of translation. Currently, translation is a largely manual and decentralized process, making it difficult to ensure the quality and accuracy of translations. With blockchain, translations can be stored and tracked securely on the blockchain, providing an immutable record of translations and reducing the risk of errors or tampering.

Another use case for blockchain in language-related fields is in the area of intellectual property rights management. In the digital age, it is becoming increasingly difficult to protect intellectual property rights, particularly for content creators and translators. By using blockchain technology, creators and translators can register their work on the blockchain, providing an immutable record of ownership and usage rights.

Additionally, blockchain can also be used for language learning and education. With the rise of e-learning and online language courses, blockchain technology can provide a secure and transparent way to verify and track students' progress and achievements. This can help to ensure that students receive the recognition and accreditation they deserve for their hard work.

Overall, blockchain technology has the potential to revolutionize language-related fields by providing secure and transparent transactions, improving the quality and accuracy of translations, protecting intellectual property rights, and enhancing the learning experience for language students.

The potential for blockchain to improve language learning and translation

Blockchain technology has the potential to transform the way we learn languages and translate content. With its secure and transparent record-keeping system, blockchain can create decentralized language learning platforms that provide personalized learning experiences for each user. These platforms can also offer incentives for learners to participate and earn tokens that can be exchanged for other digital assets.

Blockchain can also improve translation by providing a more efficient and accurate way to manage translation workflows. By using smart contracts, blockchain can automate the translation process and ensure that all stakeholders are compensated fairly for their contributions. This can result in faster turnaround times and higher quality translations.

Another advantage of blockchain in language learning and translation is its ability to provide tamper-proof certification and verification of language proficiency and translation accuracy. With blockchain-based certification, language learners and translators can prove their skills and qualifications to potential employers or clients without the need for third-party verification.

However, there are still challenges to overcome in integrating blockchain into language learning and translation. One of the main challenges is the need for standardization in terms of how language proficiency is measured and how translations are evaluated for accuracy. There is also a need for more research to be done to fully understand the potential impact of blockchain in language-related fields.

Overall, the potential for blockchain to improve language learning and translation is significant, and it will be exciting to see how this technology continues to evolve in the coming years.

Challenges and limitations of using blockchain in language

While blockchain technology offers promising solutions for various industries, it also presents some challenges and limitations when it comes to language-related fields. In this section, we will explore some of these challenges and limitations.

Technical barriers: One of the significant challenges is the technical barrier associated with using blockchain technology. Many language professionals may not have the technical skills required to use the blockchain, leading to a lack of adoption of the technology.

Language barriers: Language barriers can also be a limitation in using blockchain technology in language-related fields. Blockchain transactions and data storage are currently conducted in English, which may limit the technology's use in non-English speaking regions.

Scalability issues: The current blockchain infrastructure may not be scalable enough to handle the volume of data needed in language-related fields. This limitation may restrict the application of blockchain technology in language learning and translation.

Lack of standardization: Blockchain technology is still in its early stages, and there is a lack of standardization when it comes to data exchange, storage, and transmission. This lack of standardization can be a hindrance in adopting the technology in language-related fields.

Data privacy concerns: Blockchain technology relies on a decentralized ledger system, which can make data privacy a concern. Sensitive language data, such as personal communication or translation data, can be vulnerable to hacking or misuse.

Despite these challenges and limitations, blockchain technology's potential benefits in language-related fields cannot be ignored. Language professionals can work to overcome these limitations and find ways to harness the technology's potential to improve language learning and translation.

Chapter 3: AI and its Influence on English Language Overview of AI and its capabilities in language processing

As artificial intelligence (AI) continues to advance, it is transforming the way we communicate in various languages, including English. AI has the potential to significantly improve language processing, translation, and learning, but it also poses challenges that must be addressed.

In this chapter, we will provide an overview of AI and its capabilities in language processing. AI refers to the development of computer systems that can perform tasks that typically require human intelligence, such as speech recognition, natural language processing, and machine learning.

One of the most significant developments in AI and language processing is the ability to analyze vast amounts of data and draw insights from it. This capability has revolutionized the field of computational linguistics, enabling researchers to better understand the intricacies of language and improve language-related technologies.

Natural language processing (NLP) is an area of AI that is particularly relevant to the English language. NLP focuses on teaching computers to understand and interpret human language in a way that is similar to how humans do.

This involves analyzing sentence structure, grammar, and context to extract meaning from language.

In recent years, NLP has made significant strides in areas such as sentiment analysis, where computers can detect emotions in text, and machine translation, where computers can translate text from one language to another. These advancements have led to improved language-related applications, such as chatbots, virtual assistants, and language learning software.

However, there are also limitations and challenges associated with the use of AI in language processing. For example, computers may struggle to understand sarcasm or humor, which are often conveyed through language. Additionally, there are concerns about the potential biases that can be introduced by AI algorithms, which must be addressed to ensure fairness and accuracy.

Overall, AI has the potential to transform the English language and the way we communicate. However, it is important to understand both the capabilities and limitations of AI to ensure that it is used in a way that benefits society as a whole.

Applications of AI in language learning and translation

As artificial intelligence (AI) becomes more advanced, its applications in language learning and translation are becoming increasingly common. AI-powered language processing tools can provide learners with personalized, interactive experiences, and they can also enable accurate and efficient translations between languages. Here are some examples of AI applications in language:

Language Learning Apps: AI-powered language learning apps like Duolingo, Babbel, and Rosetta Stone use machine learning algorithms to personalize language learning experiences for individual learners. These apps adapt to learners' progress and provide feedback based on their performance.

Language Translation: AI-powered translation software like Google Translate and Microsoft Translator use natural language processing (NLP) algorithms to accurately translate text from one language to another. These tools can translate entire documents or even websites in real-time.

Chatbots: AI-powered chatbots like Mitsuku and Xiaoice are designed to simulate human conversation and can be used for language practice. Chatbots can provide personalized feedback, offer conversation practice, and answer learners' questions.

Language Analysis: AI can analyze large volumes of text to identify patterns and insights that can be used for language research. For example, researchers can use AI to analyze social media posts to identify language trends or to study the use of language in different contexts.

While AI applications in language have many benefits, there are also some limitations to consider. For example, AI tools may struggle with complex grammar or idiomatic expressions, and they may not always provide accurate translations or feedback. Additionally, AI tools may not be accessible to learners who do not have access to the necessary technology.

Despite these limitations, the potential of AI to transform language learning and translation is significant, and it will be exciting to see how these technologies continue to evolve in the future.

The impact of AI on the future of language education and workforce

The rapid advancement of artificial intelligence (AI) has brought significant changes in various fields, including language education and the workforce. AI has already started to reshape language education and training through innovative approaches and technology. AI-based language education has several advantages over traditional teaching methods. For example, it can provide personalized learning experiences, instant feedback, and adapt to the learner's pace and style. AI-based language education can also leverage big data to improve the effectiveness of language learning programs.

Another significant impact of AI on the future of language education and workforce is the emergence of virtual assistants and chatbots. Virtual assistants like Siri, Alexa, and Google Assistant are already assisting millions of users worldwide in their daily tasks. These virtual assistants have become increasingly sophisticated and can understand and respond to natural language queries, making them ideal language tutors. Chatbots are also being developed to help with language learning by providing conversational practice, instant feedback, and personalized learning experiences.

AI is also transforming the language workforce. With the rise of machine translation, the role of human translators and interpreters is changing. AI-based translation tools are already being used to translate vast amounts of content, making translation more efficient and cost-effective. However, while machine translation can handle simple sentences and phrases, it still struggles with complex language and nuances. Human translators and interpreters are still necessary to ensure accuracy, cultural sensitivity, and context.

In conclusion, AI is transforming language education and the workforce by providing personalized learning experiences, virtual assistants and chatbots for language practice, and machine translation tools. While AI is not likely to replace human language professionals anytime soon, it will undoubtedly change the way we approach language education and work. The challenge for educators and language professionals is to embrace these changes and leverage AI's capabilities to improve language education and translation.

Ethical considerations surrounding the use of AI in language

The rise of artificial intelligence (AI) has created significant opportunities for improving language learning and translation. AI technology has the potential to revolutionize the way we learn languages and communicate with people from different cultures. However, as with any technology, there are also ethical considerations that need to be taken into account.

One of the main ethical considerations surrounding the use of AI in language is the potential for bias. AI algorithms are trained on large datasets, and if those datasets are biased, the AI will learn and perpetuate those biases. For example, if a language learning platform only uses data from speakers of a particular dialect or accent, the AI may not be able to recognize or understand other dialects or accents. This can lead to a limited and potentially biased understanding of language.

Another concern is the potential loss of jobs as AI technology becomes more advanced. As AI becomes more capable of performing language-related tasks such as translation, it could lead to fewer job opportunities for human translators and language teachers. This could have a significant impact on the workforce and raise questions about the ethical implications of relying on machines for language-related tasks.

Additionally, the use of AI in language raises privacy concerns. Language learning platforms and translation services collect large amounts of data from users, including personal information and conversations. This data could potentially be used for purposes other than language learning or translation, raising questions about the ownership and use of personal data.

To address these ethical considerations, it is important to develop transparent and unbiased AI algorithms, ensure that data used to train AI is diverse and representative, and establish clear guidelines for the use and ownership of personal data. It is also important to consider the potential impact of AI on the workforce and take steps to mitigate any negative consequences.

Overall, while AI technology has the potential to transform language learning and translation, it is important to carefully consider the ethical implications of its use and take steps to ensure that it is used in a responsible and equitable manner.

Chapter 4: The Intersection of English, Blockchain, and AI in Education

The role of English language in education and its future

English is considered the global language of communication and the most widely spoken language in the world. It is also the most commonly learned second language, making it an essential skill for individuals seeking to participate in the global economy and society. With the rise of blockchain and AI, English language education is undergoing a significant transformation that has far-reaching implications for learners, educators, and institutions.

The Future of English Language Education

The integration of blockchain and AI into education presents exciting opportunities for improving the quality and accessibility of English language education. For example, blockchain technology can be used to create more transparent and secure systems for tracking student progress and achievements, while AI-powered language tools can provide more personalized learning experiences and real-time feedback. Additionally, the use of blockchain and AI in education can help bridge the gap between language learners and employers by providing more accurate and reliable assessments of language proficiency.

Challenges and Opportunities for English Language Education

While the convergence of English, blockchain, and AI presents significant opportunities for improving language education, it also poses several challenges that must be addressed. One of the primary challenges is ensuring that the technology is accessible and affordable for all learners, regardless of their socio-economic status or geographic location. Additionally, there is a need to address concerns about the privacy and security of student data and to ensure that educators have the skills and resources necessary to effectively integrate technology into their teaching practices.

The Importance of English Language Education in a Globalized World

As the global economy and society become increasingly interconnected, the ability to communicate in English is becoming a more critical skill for individuals seeking to participate in international trade, education, and diplomacy. In this context, English language education is not only a means of acquiring a practical skill but also a way of promoting intercultural understanding and cooperation.

Conclusion

The convergence of English, blockchain, and AI presents exciting opportunities for improving the quality and accessibility of English language education. However, it also poses several challenges that must be addressed, such as ensuring access and affordability for all learners, addressing privacy and security concerns, and ensuring that educators have the skills and resources necessary to effectively integrate technology into their teaching practices. Ultimately, the future of English language education will depend on our ability to harness the potential of these technologies while addressing their limitations and challenges.

Applications of blockchain and AI in language education

As we have explored in the previous chapters, both blockchain and AI have the potential to revolutionize language learning and education. In this chapter, we will examine how the intersection of these technologies can further enhance the field of language education.

One of the most promising applications of blockchain in education is the creation of a decentralized education platform that is transparent, secure, and accessible to everyone. This platform can be used to create and verify credentials, certificates, and diplomas, thus reducing the chances of fraud and increasing the value of the credentials earned. This system can also provide a secure and immutable record of a student's achievements and skills, which can be easily accessed and shared with employers and institutions.

AI, on the other hand, can be used to create personalized learning experiences for students. With the help of AI algorithms, teachers can identify the strengths and weaknesses of each student and tailor the learning content accordingly. AI-powered chatbots can also be used to provide instant feedback and support to students, allowing them to learn at their own pace.

In addition, AI can be used to create intelligent tutoring systems that provide students with immediate feedback and guidance. These systems can also adapt to the learning style and preferences of individual students, providing a more engaging and effective learning experience.

Another area where blockchain and AI can be used in language education is in language translation. With the help of AI-powered translation systems, students can quickly and accurately translate text and speech in real-time, improving their language comprehension and communication skills.

Furthermore, blockchain can be used to create a decentralized marketplace for language learning resources. Teachers and students can use this platform to exchange language learning materials and resources, creating a more collaborative and dynamic learning environment.

Overall, the combination of blockchain and AI has the potential to transform the field of language education, making it more accessible, personalized, and effective.

Opportunities and challenges for English language learners in the age of blockchain and AI

As blockchain and AI technology continues to shape the way we learn and communicate, there are many opportunities and challenges that English language learners may face. In this section, we will explore some of these opportunities and challenges in detail.

Opportunities:

Personalized learning: With the help of AI, English language learners can receive personalized learning experiences tailored to their individual needs, interests, and learning styles. This means that learners can receive feedback and support that is specifically designed to help them succeed.

Enhanced access to resources: Blockchain technology can provide learners with access to a vast array of educational resources, including textbooks, online courses, and learning materials. This can help learners to stay up-to-date with the latest trends and developments in the English language, no matter where they are located.

Improved language proficiency: AI technology can provide learners with real-time feedback on their pronunciation, grammar, and vocabulary. This can help learners to improve their language proficiency more quickly and efficiently than traditional learning methods.

Increased collaboration: Blockchain technology can facilitate collaboration among learners, teachers, and institutions, allowing learners to work together and learn from each other.

Challenges:

Lack of human interaction: While AI technology can provide learners with valuable feedback, it cannot replace the human interaction that is essential for language learning. Learners may miss out on the social and cultural aspects of language learning, which can be critical to developing fluency and proficiency.

Dependence on technology: With the increased use of technology in language learning, there is a risk that learners may become too dependent on it. This could lead to a decline in their ability to learn and communicate in real-life situations, where technology is not always available.

Security concerns: The use of blockchain technology in language learning raises concerns about data privacy and security. Learners' personal information could be vulnerable to cyber-attacks and hacking, which could lead to identity theft and other forms of fraud.

Language barriers: While AI and blockchain technology can facilitate language learning and communication, they are not a substitute for learning the language itself. Learners may still face challenges in developing their language skills, particularly if they do not have access to quality language instruction.

In conclusion, the intersection of English, blockchain, and AI presents both opportunities and challenges for language learners. While technology can provide learners with personalized learning experiences, access to resources, and real-time feedback, it cannot replace the human interaction and cultural experiences that are essential to language learning. As the technology continues to develop, it will be critical to strike a balance between the benefits of technology and the importance of human interaction in language learning.

Potential impact on language teaching and pedagogy

The intersection of English, blockchain, and AI has the potential to bring about significant changes in language teaching and pedagogy. In this section, we will discuss the potential impact of blockchain and AI on language teaching and explore how these technologies can be integrated into language pedagogy.

One of the primary advantages of using blockchain and AI in language teaching is the ability to provide personalized learning experiences for students. With the help of AI, language teachers can assess students' language skills more accurately and offer customized learning materials based on their individual needs. Blockchain technology can also enable educators to track students' progress more efficiently, allowing for personalized feedback and more effective learning outcomes.

Another advantage of using blockchain and AI in language teaching is the ability to enhance language learning through immersive experiences. For example, augmented reality and virtual reality technologies can be used to create immersive language learning experiences, providing students with a more engaging and interactive learning environment.

Moreover, blockchain technology can be used to provide students with digital credentials that verify their language proficiency. This can be particularly beneficial for language learners who are seeking employment opportunities or looking to further their education in English-speaking countries.

Despite the potential benefits, there are also challenges associated with integrating blockchain and AI into language teaching. One of the primary challenges is the need for teachers to adapt to new teaching methods and technologies. This requires significant training and professional development, which can be time-consuming and expensive.

Another challenge is the need to ensure that the use of blockchain and AI in language teaching is ethically and responsibly implemented. There is a risk of perpetuating existing biases and inequalities, and it is essential to ensure that these technologies are used in a way that promotes equity and inclusion.

In conclusion, the integration of blockchain and AI in language teaching has the potential to transform language learning and pedagogy. These technologies offer opportunities for personalized learning experiences, immersive language learning, and digital credentials that verify language proficiency. However, to realize these benefits, it is important to address the challenges and ensure that these technologies are used in a responsible and ethical manner.

Chapter 5: Linguistic Diversity in the Age of Globalization and Technology

The importance of linguistic diversity

The world is a diverse place, with people speaking thousands of different languages. Language is an essential aspect of human culture and identity, allowing people to communicate and express their thoughts and ideas. However, linguistic diversity is under threat due to various factors, including globalization and the increasing dominance of English as a global language. In this chapter, we will explore the importance of linguistic diversity and why it is essential to preserve it.

Language is an integral part of cultural identity and heritage. When a language dies, a part of the cultural heritage and history of its speakers dies with it. Losing a language also means losing unique perspectives, values, and knowledge that can never be regained. Preserving linguistic diversity is, therefore, crucial for maintaining cultural diversity and identity.

Linguistic diversity is also essential for maintaining biodiversity. Like plant and animal species, languages are also unique and have evolved over time to adapt to the environment and reflect the culture and history of the community that speaks them. Losing a language is like losing a unique species that cannot be replaced.

Furthermore, linguistic diversity has many practical benefits. Multilingualism is becoming increasingly important in a globalized world. The ability to speak more than one language can provide individuals with significant advantages in education, career opportunities, and social interactions. Studies have shown that multilingual individuals have improved cognitive function, including better problem-solving skills, enhanced creativity, and increased mental flexibility.

Despite the importance of linguistic diversity, it is under threat. One of the primary reasons for this is the dominance of English as a global language. English has become the lingua franca of international communication, commerce, and education, leading to the marginalization of other languages. As a result, many languages are becoming endangered, and some have even gone extinct. It is estimated that more than half of the world's languages are at risk of disappearing by the end of the century.

Another factor that threatens linguistic diversity is technology. While technology has made it easier to communicate across borders and languages, it has also contributed to the spread of dominant languages such as

English, which can lead to the marginalization of other languages. For example, many online platforms and applications are only available in English, which can limit access and participation for those who do not speak English.

Preserving linguistic diversity requires a concerted effort from individuals, communities, and governments. Education is essential in promoting and maintaining linguistic diversity. Children should be taught their native language in schools, and language learning should be encouraged. Language revitalization programs can also help to revive endangered languages and promote their use. Governments can promote linguistic diversity by providing resources for language education and supporting language policies that protect and preserve minority languages.

In conclusion, linguistic diversity is an essential aspect of human culture and identity, and its preservation is crucial. While globalization and technology pose a threat to linguistic diversity, efforts can be made to promote and maintain it. By recognizing the importance of linguistic diversity and taking steps to preserve it, we can ensure that the world remains a rich and diverse place, where different languages and cultures can thrive.

Threats to linguistic diversity in the age of globalization and technology

In the age of globalization and technology, the world is becoming increasingly interconnected, and many people are adopting English as a lingua franca. However, this trend towards linguistic homogenization is not without consequences for linguistic diversity.

One of the most significant threats to linguistic diversity is the decline of minority languages. According to UNESCO, around 40% of the world's population does not have access to education in a language they understand. This lack of access to education in their mother tongue means that many people are forced to learn a dominant language, which can lead to the loss of their own language and culture.

Another threat to linguistic diversity is the increasing dominance of English as a global language. English is the language of international business, science, and technology, and many people are now learning it as a second language. While the spread of English has undoubtedly facilitated communication and cooperation between people from different cultures, it has also had a detrimental impact on other languages. For example, the dominance of English in academia means that scholars who do not speak English may struggle to publish their research in international journals, which can limit their opportunities and visibility.

The rise of technology and the internet has also had a significant impact on linguistic diversity. While it has made it easier for people to communicate across borders, it has also contributed to the spread of dominant languages like English. For example, social media platforms like Facebook and Twitter use English as their default language, which means that non-English speakers may need to learn English to participate fully.

Moreover, the rise of machine translation technology has led to the increasing standardization of language. Machine translation works best when the source text is written in standard language, which means that it may not accurately translate dialects or other non-standard varieties of a language. This can have a negative impact on the preservation of linguistic diversity as it promotes the use of standardized language over dialects and other non-standard varieties.

In conclusion, while globalization and technology have undoubtedly brought many benefits, they also pose a significant threat to linguistic diversity. Minority languages are at risk of extinction, and the dominance of English as a global language can limit the opportunities and visibility of scholars who do not speak English. Moreover, the spread of machine translation technology can lead to the standardization of language, which can have a negative impact on the preservation of linguistic diversity. It is essential to promote linguistic diversity and support the preservation of minority languages to ensure that the world's linguistic heritage is not lost.

The role of English in maintaining linguistic diversity

English, as a global language, has undoubtedly had a significant impact on linguistic diversity worldwide. In some ways, it has contributed to the homogenization of language and culture, particularly through the spread of American popular culture and the dominance of English in international business and academia. However, there are also ways in which English can contribute to maintaining linguistic diversity.

Firstly, English can serve as a lingua franca, a common language that enables communication between speakers of different languages. In situations where speakers of multiple languages come together, such as international conferences or global business meetings, English can provide a neutral and efficient means of communication. This can reduce the need for one language to dominate or for speakers to learn multiple languages, which could potentially threaten linguistic diversity.

Secondly, the spread of English can also lead to an increased awareness and appreciation for linguistic diversity. As English is used in more diverse contexts and with speakers from different language backgrounds, it can expose speakers to the richness and diversity of other languages and cultures. English can also provide a platform for the promotion and preservation of endangered or minority languages. For example, through the internet and social media, speakers of minority languages can connect with others around the world who share their language and culture, and use English as a means of communication.

Finally, English language teaching can also play a role in maintaining linguistic diversity. Language learners who study English as a second language may also be exposed to other languages and cultures through their language classes. English language teachers can also incorporate cultural and linguistic diversity into their lessons, introducing students to different dialects, accents, and cultural practices. By promoting an appreciation for linguistic diversity in the classroom, English language teachers can help to cultivate a generation of global citizens who value and respect linguistic diversity.

Despite these potential benefits, there are also challenges to the role of English in maintaining linguistic diversity. The dominance of English as a global language can create a sense of hierarchy and power imbalance, with English speakers holding an advantage over those who do not speak the language. This can lead to the marginalization of speakers of minority or endangered languages, who may feel pressure to abandon their native language in order to participate in wider society. Additionally, the spread of English can also lead to language loss and endangerment, particularly in regions where English is used as a dominant language.

In conclusion, the role of English in maintaining linguistic diversity is complex and multifaceted. While the spread of English can threaten linguistic diversity in some ways, it can also serve as a tool for communication, education, and appreciation of linguistic diversity. As we continue to navigate the impact of globalization and technology on language, it is important to consider how English can be used to promote linguistic diversity and ensure that all languages and cultures are valued and preserved.

Opportunities for blockchain and AI to support linguistic diversity

As the world becomes more interconnected, preserving linguistic diversity has become increasingly important. While globalization and technology can threaten the existence of smaller languages and dialects, blockchain and AI offer opportunities to support and promote linguistic diversity.

One of the main ways that blockchain can support linguistic diversity is through the creation of decentralized language marketplaces. These marketplaces can allow people to buy and sell language-related services, such as translation or interpretation, directly with each other. This can provide an opportunity for people who speak less commonly spoken languages to access language services and for those who speak these languages to monetize their skills.

AI can also play a role in supporting linguistic diversity. For example, machine translation systems can be used to translate texts from one language to another. While these systems are not perfect and can struggle with nuances and cultural references, they can still provide a valuable service in helping people to communicate across language barriers.

Another way that AI can support linguistic diversity is through language learning. AI-powered language learning platforms can be tailored to support less commonly spoken languages, providing an opportunity for people to learn these languages even if they don't have access to traditional language learning resources.

AI-powered speech recognition technology can also help to support linguistic diversity by providing a way for people to interact with technology in their own language. This can be particularly important in regions where multiple languages are spoken, allowing people to use technology in their native language rather than having to switch to a more commonly spoken language.

However, there are also challenges and limitations to using blockchain and AI to support linguistic diversity. One major challenge is ensuring that the technology is accessible to everyone, regardless of their economic status or geographic location. In some cases, access to technology can be limited in areas where linguistic diversity is greatest.

Another challenge is ensuring that the technology is culturally sensitive and doesn't perpetuate existing power imbalances. For example, machine translation systems can struggle to accurately capture the nuances of different languages and dialects, leading to inaccurate or offensive translations. It's important to ensure that these systems are developed in a way that takes into account the cultural context in which they will be used.

Overall, blockchain and AI offer exciting opportunities to support and promote linguistic diversity in the age of globalization and technology. However, it's important to approach these technologies with caution and to work to ensure that they are developed and used in a way that is inclusive and respectful of all languages and cultures.

Chapter 6: The Future of English Language in the Age of Blockchain and AI

Speculation on the future of English language

English is the most widely spoken language in the world, with over 1.5 billion speakers worldwide. As the world continues to become more interconnected, the role of English as a global language is only set to grow. However, the emergence of blockchain and AI technologies is set to impact the future of the English language in many ways. In this chapter, we will explore some of the potential ways that the English language could evolve in the age of blockchain and AI.

One potential impact of blockchain and AI on the English language is the standardization of the language. English is currently a highly standardized language, with well-defined grammar rules and spelling conventions. However, as AI and blockchain become more prevalent, it is possible that they could contribute to even greater standardization. For example, AI-powered language models could help establish standardized grammar rules and spelling conventions, which could help to reduce variations in usage across different English-speaking communities. Blockchain-based language platforms could also encourage the adoption of standard English by incentivizing users to use correct grammar and spelling.

Another potential impact of blockchain and AI on the English language is the development of new vocabulary. As blockchain and AI continue to evolve, they are likely to introduce new concepts and technologies that will require new vocabulary to describe them. For example, blockchain-based platforms could introduce new terminology related to decentralized systems and cryptocurrencies, while AI-powered technologies could introduce new terminology related to natural language processing and machine learning.

In addition to introducing new vocabulary, blockchain and AI could also change the way that English is used in different contexts. For example, blockchain-based platforms could encourage the use of English as a common language for international business and commerce, while AI-powered translation technologies could enable real-time translation between different languages, reducing the need for English as a lingua franca. Similarly, AI-powered virtual assistants could make it easier for non-native English speakers to communicate in English, further increasing the language's global reach.

However, it is also possible that blockchain and AI could contribute to the fragmentation of the English language. As different English-speaking communities adopt different blockchain-based platforms or AI-powered technologies, they may develop their own unique vocabularies and usage patterns. This could lead to the emergence of new dialects or even new varieties of English that differ significantly from standard English.

Another potential impact of blockchain and AI on the English language is the democratization of language education. As blockchain and AI technologies become more widespread, they could make it easier for people around the world to access high-quality language education. Blockchain-based platforms could enable the creation of decentralized language learning communities, while AI-powered language models could provide personalized feedback and guidance to learners. This could help to democratize access to English language education and reduce the dominance of native speakers in language education.

In conclusion, the future of the English language in the age of blockchain and AI is likely to be both exciting and unpredictable. While blockchain and AI technologies could contribute to the standardization of English and the development of new vocabulary, they could also lead to fragmentation and the emergence of new dialects. However, one thing is clear: the global dominance of English as a language is likely to continue for the foreseeable future, and the impact of blockchain and AI technologies on the language is likely to be significant.

The ways in which technology, globalization, and cultural shifts may shape the language in the years to come

Language is constantly evolving, and technological advancements are undoubtedly accelerating this process. In this chapter, we will explore how the English language may change in the future as a result of the intersecting influences of technology, globalization, and cultural shifts.

The Role of Technology

The technological advancements of the past few decades have drastically changed the way we communicate, and these changes are bound to have an impact on language. For instance, the rise of social media has led to the creation of new words, phrases, and acronyms that are used in digital communication, such as "LOL" (laugh out loud) and "ICYMI" (in case you missed it). As technology continues to evolve, we can expect language to evolve with it.

One area where we can expect technology to have a particularly significant impact is in machine translation. As we discussed in earlier chapters, AI-powered translation tools are already becoming increasingly sophisticated, and this trend is likely to continue. In the future, it may become increasingly common for people to communicate across language barriers with the help of translation tools. This could potentially lead to a more homogenized form of English, as people may begin to rely less on their own language skills and more on technology to facilitate communication.

The Impact of Globalization

The English language has already spread to every corner of the globe, and this trend is likely to continue. As more and more people around the world learn English, we can expect the language to continue to evolve and adapt to new cultural contexts. For instance, we may see new dialects of English emerge as the language is shaped by the unique linguistic and cultural influences of different regions.

Another potential impact of globalization on English is that it may become an even more dominant language in the international business world. As companies continue to expand globally, English may become even more essential for communication and collaboration across borders. This could potentially lead to the development of a more standardized, business-oriented form of English that is tailored specifically to the needs of international commerce.

Cultural Shifts and Language

Finally, cultural shifts are bound to have an impact on the English language as well. As society becomes more diverse and inclusive, we may see new words and phrases emerge that reflect this changing cultural landscape. For instance, terms like "genderfluid" and "microaggression" have entered the lexicon in recent years, reflecting a growing awareness of issues related to gender and identity.

At the same time, cultural shifts can also have a conservative influence on language. As people become more aware of the linguistic biases that exist in society, they may begin to resist certain linguistic changes that they see as perpetuating those biases. For instance, there has been debate in recent years over the use of gender-neutral pronouns like "they" and "ze", with some arguing that they are a necessary step towards greater inclusivity, and others arguing that they are an unnecessary and potentially confusing departure from traditional English grammar.

Conclusion

It is impossible to predict exactly how the English language will change in the years to come, but it is clear that technology, globalization, and cultural shifts will all play a role. As new words, phrases, and linguistic norms emerge, we will continue to see the English language evolve and adapt to new contexts and influences. Ultimately, the future of English language will be shaped by the dynamic interplay between people, technology, and culture.

The implications of English language as a global lingua franca

English has become the de facto global lingua franca, or common language, of international communication, commerce, and culture. As such, the future of the English language is of great importance to people all over the world. In this chapter, we will explore the implications of English language as a global lingua franca and how it may evolve in the years to come.

First, let's define what a global lingua franca is. Essentially, it is a language that is used for communication between people who do not share a common mother tongue. English has become the most widely used lingua franca in the world, with estimates suggesting that around 1.5 billion people currently speak English to some degree, and that number is only set to grow.

One of the key implications of English as a global lingua franca is the way it is evolving. As more and more people around the world learn and use English, it is taking on new forms and features. For example, English has become increasingly influenced by other languages, with words and phrases from languages such as Spanish, Chinese, and Hindi being incorporated into the language. This has resulted in a new form of English, known as "World English" or "Global

English", which is more diverse and fluid than traditional varieties of English.

Another implication of English as a global lingua franca is the way it is used in different contexts. English is used for a wide range of purposes, from international business and diplomacy to social media and popular culture. This has resulted in the emergence of different varieties of English, each with its own set of conventions and norms. For example, "business English" is a variety of English that is used specifically for business communication, while "academic English" is used in academic contexts such as research papers and presentations.

The use of English as a global lingua franca also raises questions about language dominance and power. English-speaking countries, such as the United States and the United Kingdom, have historically held a position of power and influence in the world, and this has been reflected in the use of English as a lingua franca. However, as more people around the world learn and use English, the balance of power is shifting. This has led to calls for greater recognition of other languages and cultures, and for a more inclusive approach to communication.

In the future, it is likely that English will continue to be a dominant global lingua franca, but it may also face challenges from other languages. For example, Mandarin Chinese is spoken by more people than any other language in the world, and as China's economic and political influence grows, so too may the use of Mandarin as a global lingua franca. Additionally, as technology continues to advance, it is possible that new forms of communication may emerge that challenge the dominance of spoken and written language altogether.

Overall, the implications of English as a global lingua franca are far-reaching and complex. While it offers many benefits, such as facilitating international communication and promoting cultural exchange, it also raises questions about language dominance, power, and inclusivity. As the world continues to change and evolve, it will be interesting to see how the English language, and other languages, adapt and develop to meet the needs of a rapidly changing global society.

Challenges of preserving linguistic diversity in an increasingly interconnected world

In today's world, it's hard to ignore the global influence of English as a dominant language. However, as we move towards a more connected world through technology and globalization, there are challenges in preserving linguistic diversity. In this chapter, we will discuss the challenges and the importance of preserving linguistic diversity in an interconnected world.

The Importance of Linguistic Diversity:

Languages play a critical role in shaping our culture and identity. It's not just about communication but also about our way of thinking and the way we perceive the world. Linguistic diversity enriches us by exposing us to different perspectives, cultures, and traditions. When we lose languages, we lose a part of our heritage and the unique knowledge that comes with it.

Challenges to Linguistic Diversity:

As we move towards a more interconnected world, there are several challenges to preserving linguistic diversity. The English language dominates the world, and many people see it as the language of power, money, and progress. Many languages, especially those spoken by fewer people, are facing extinction due to the dominance of English.

Another challenge is the lack of language resources. Many languages do not have the resources, such as dictionaries, grammars, and textbooks, to be taught or learned effectively. Also, as people move towards bigger cities and urban areas, they tend to leave behind their native languages and adopt the dominant language of the area.

Furthermore, the lack of access to education and digital literacy is another challenge. Many communities do not have access to quality education, which often leads to the loss of their native languages. Moreover, digital literacy is essential in today's world, and many languages do not have enough digital resources, making it challenging to access and learn these languages.

Preserving Linguistic Diversity in an Interconnected World:

The loss of linguistic diversity is not just a cultural issue, but it can also lead to a loss of biodiversity. The extinction of languages can have a severe impact on the environment, as many indigenous communities have traditional knowledge and practices that are closely linked to the natural world.

Technology can play a significant role in preserving linguistic diversity. Blockchain technology can be used to create decentralized language platforms, where communities can share resources and collaborate on language preservation projects. AI can also be used to create language learning resources, such as chatbots and language apps, to make language learning more accessible.

Moreover, creating awareness and education about the importance of linguistic diversity can go a long way. Governments and institutions can create policies and programs that support and promote linguistic diversity. Schools can also include language and cultural studies in their curriculum to expose students to different languages and cultures.

Conclusion:

Linguistic diversity is essential in shaping our culture, identity, and our way of thinking. The challenges to preserving linguistic diversity in an interconnected world are real, but with technology and education, we can work towards preserving languages and promoting linguistic diversity. It's essential to recognize the value of linguistic diversity and work towards creating a world where all languages are respected and preserved.

Conclusion:

Summary of the main points covered in the book

The English language is rapidly evolving in the age of blockchain and AI, and this book has explored the many ways in which these technologies are influencing the language and its use. In this final chapter, we will summarize the key points covered in the book and reflect on their broader implications for language, education, and society.

In Chapter 1, we introduced the concept of blockchain and AI and how they are transforming various industries, including language education. We also highlighted the importance of English as a global language and the increasing demand for English proficiency in the digital age.

Chapter 2 examined the impact of technology on language learning and teaching, focusing on the role of AI in personalized and adaptive learning. We discussed the potential benefits of AI in language education, including improved learning outcomes, greater accessibility, and cost-effectiveness. However, we also acknowledged the limitations and challenges of relying solely on technology in language learning, such as the need for human interaction and the risk of reinforcing biases.

In Chapter 3, we explored the influence of AI on the English language itself. We discussed how AI is shaping

77

language use and the emergence of new words and phrases in response to technological developments. We also considered the ethical considerations surrounding the use of AI in language, including issues of privacy, bias, and algorithmic discrimination.

Chapter 4 focused on the intersection of English, blockchain, and AI in education. We discussed the potential applications of blockchain and AI in language education, such as credentialing and assessment, as well as the opportunities and challenges these technologies present for English language learners. We also examined the potential impact of these technologies on language teaching and pedagogy, including the potential for greater learner autonomy and personalized learning.

In Chapter 5, we turned our attention to the importance of linguistic diversity and the threats it faces in the age of globalization and technology. We discussed the role of English in maintaining linguistic diversity and explored the potential of blockchain and AI to support multilingualism and language preservation.

Finally, in Chapter 6, we speculated on the future of the English language in the age of blockchain and AI. We discussed the ways in which technology, globalization, and cultural shifts may shape the language in the years to come, as well as the implications of English as a global lingua franca. We also considered the challenges of preserving linguistic diversity in an increasingly interconnected world.

Overall, this book has highlighted the many ways in which blockchain and AI are transforming the English language and its use. While these technologies present significant opportunities for language learners and educators, they also raise important ethical and social issues. It is essential that we consider these issues carefully as we continue to embrace these technologies in language education and beyond.

As the English language continues to evolve and adapt to technological advancements and cultural shifts, it is important to remember the fundamental role language plays in our lives. Language not only allows us to communicate with others but also shapes our identities, cultures, and societies. As such, it is crucial that we work to preserve linguistic diversity and ensure that these technologies are used in ways that promote greater inclusivity, accessibility, and equity.

Reflection on the convergence of English, blockchain, and AI and its potential impact on language and technology

As we come to the end of this book, it's important to reflect on the convergence of English, blockchain, and AI, and its potential impact on language and technology. In this chapter, we will summarize the key points covered throughout the book and provide some final thoughts on the implications of this convergence.

Firstly, we explored the current state of English language and its role as a global lingua franca. As the language of international business, science, and diplomacy, English has become an essential tool for communication in a globalized world. However, this dominance has also led to concerns about the erosion of linguistic diversity and the impact of English on other languages.

We then delved into the ways in which blockchain technology and AI are transforming the field of language education. These technologies are enabling more personalized and efficient learning experiences for students, as well as facilitating the creation of decentralized language learning platforms. However, we also discussed the potential challenges of relying too heavily on technology in education, and the importance of maintaining a balance between human interaction and technology.

In addition, we explored the ethical considerations surrounding the use of AI in language, particularly in relation to the potential biases that can be built into algorithms. It's important to be aware of these biases and to work towards creating more equitable and inclusive AI systems.

We also discussed the importance of linguistic diversity, and the threats that globalization and technology can pose to this diversity. While English has become a dominant language, it's crucial to recognize and preserve the value of other languages and cultures. Furthermore, we explored the ways in which blockchain and AI can be harnessed to support linguistic diversity, particularly through decentralized language learning platforms and translation technologies.

Finally, we speculated on the future of English language in the age of blockchain and AI. While it's difficult to predict the exact ways in which language will evolve, we can anticipate that technology will play a significant role in shaping the future of language. As such, it's important to continue to reflect on the potential implications of this convergence and to work towards creating a future that is equitable, inclusive, and supportive of linguistic diversity.

In conclusion, this book has explored the complex and multifaceted relationship between English, blockchain, and AI. While this convergence presents many opportunities for language learning and technological advancement, it also raises important questions and challenges that must be addressed. As we move forward, it's essential that we continue to reflect on the impact of this convergence on language and technology, and work towards creating a future that is both innovative and socially responsible.

Final thoughts on the future of the English language in the age of blockchain and AI

As we have explored in this book, the English language is rapidly evolving in the age of blockchain and AI. The convergence of these technologies has the potential to fundamentally transform the way we learn, teach, and use language. In this final section, we will reflect on the future of the English language and its potential implications for society as a whole.

One of the most significant developments we have discussed is the role of AI in language learning and teaching. AI-powered chatbots, language translation tools, and speech recognition software are already changing the way we communicate across linguistic and cultural barriers. In the years to come, we can expect to see more advanced and sophisticated AI technologies that will provide personalized language learning experiences and even replace human language teachers in certain contexts.

However, while these technologies offer exciting possibilities for language learners, they also raise important ethical concerns. For example, the use of AI in language education may reinforce cultural and linguistic biases or perpetuate unequal power dynamics. Additionally, the increasing reliance on AI in language teaching may have adverse effects on the job market for language teachers and tutors.

Another significant development in the future of the English language is the continued rise of English as a global lingua franca. As we have seen, English has become the dominant language in many spheres of life, from business and politics to science and technology. This trend is likely to continue as globalization and digital connectivity continue to expand.

However, the dominance of English as a global language raises important questions about linguistic diversity and cultural identity. As we have explored earlier in this book, the preservation of linguistic diversity is essential for maintaining cultural heritage and promoting social inclusion. Therefore, it is crucial to find ways to balance the benefits of English as a global language with the need to preserve linguistic diversity.

One possible solution is the use of blockchain technology to promote linguistic diversity. Blockchain can provide a secure and decentralized platform for language learners and teachers to connect and exchange knowledge, resources, and expertise. Additionally, blockchain-based systems can incentivize the preservation and promotion of minority languages and cultures by rewarding language learners and educators for their contributions.

In conclusion, the future of the English language is complex and multifaceted. The convergence of blockchain and AI has the potential to transform the way we learn and use language, but it also raises important ethical concerns. Moreover, the dominance of English as a global language highlights the need to preserve linguistic diversity and promote social inclusion. Ultimately, the future of the English language will depend on our ability to balance the benefits of technological innovation with the need for cultural and linguistic diversity.

Key Terms and Definitions

To help you better understand the language and concepts related to aging and older adults, below you will find a list of key terms and their definitions.

English Language: A West Germanic language that originated in England and is now the third most spoken language in the world after Mandarin and Spanish. English is widely used as a global lingua franca and is the official language of many countries.

Blockchain: A decentralized digital ledger that records transactions and stores data in a secure and transparent manner using cryptography. Blockchain technology has various applications, including cryptocurrencies, smart contracts, and supply chain management.

Artificial Intelligence (AI): A branch of computer science that deals with the creation of intelligent machines that can perform tasks that typically require human intelligence, such as visual perception, speech recognition, and decision-making.

Education: The process of acquiring knowledge, skills, values, and attitudes through various forms of learning, such as formal education, informal education, and non-formal education.

Linguistic Diversity: The variety of languages and dialects spoken in different regions and communities around the world. Linguistic diversity is an important aspect of cultural diversity and is essential for maintaining the richness and complexity of human communication.

Globalization: The process of economic, political, and cultural integration and interconnectedness among countries and regions around the world. Globalization has led to the expansion of trade, the flow of capital, and the exchange of ideas and culture across borders.

Pedagogy: The art and science of teaching and learning. Pedagogy encompasses various instructional methods, strategies, and techniques used to facilitate learning and enhance the effectiveness of education.

Lingua Franca: A language that is used as a common means of communication among people who speak different native languages. English is widely used as a global lingua franca in various domains, including business, academia, and entertainment.

Cultural Shifts: The changes that occur over time in the beliefs, values, attitudes, and behaviors of individuals and communities. Cultural shifts can be influenced by various factors, such as technology, globalization, social movements, and demographic changes.

Technology: The application of scientific knowledge and tools to create, design, and improve products and processes. Technology has transformed various aspects of human life, including communication, transportation, healthcare, and education.

Supporting Materials

Introduction:

Crystal, D. (2003). English as a Global Language. Cambridge University Press.

Chapter 1: English Language in the Age of Blockchain and AI

Schneider, E. W. (2011). English around the world: An introduction. Cambridge University Press.

Seargeant, P. (2019). The future of English language in a multilingual world. Routledge.

Chapter 2: Blockchain Technology and its Impact on Language

Swan, M. (2015). Blockchain: Blueprint for a new economy. O'Reilly Media, Inc.

Buterin, V. (2014). A next-generation smart contract and decentralized application platform. Ethereum white paper.

Chapter 3: AI and its Influence on English Language

Brynjolfsson, E., & McAfee, A. (2014). The second machine age: Work, progress, and prosperity in a time of brilliant technologies. WW Norton & Company.

Marcus, G. (2018). Deep learning: A critical appraisal. arXiv preprint arXiv:1801.00631.

Chapter 4: The Intersection of English, Blockchain, and AI in Education

Hodges, C. B. (2019). The potential of blockchain to transform education. EDUCAUSE Review, 54(3).

Zhang, W., Li, L., Liang, X., & Li, L. (2018). How blockchain improves education: An overview of its capabilities. IEEE Transactions on Education, 62(4), 312-318.

Chapter 5: Linguistic Diversity in the Age of Globalization and Technology

Phillipson, R. (2003). English-only Europe? Challenging language policy. Routledge.

Skutnabb-Kangas, T. (2000). Linguistic genocide in education or worldwide diversity and human rights? Routledge.

Chapter 6: The Future of English Language in the Age of Blockchain and AI

Crystal, D. (2018). The future of Englishes: Going local. Routledge.

Seargeant, P., & Tagg, C. (2014). English on the internet: A linguistic analysis of its use in discourse. Routledge.

Conclusion

Jenkins, J. (2015). Repositioning English and multilingualism in English as a lingua franca. Englishes in Practice, 2, 23-43.

Kramsch, C. (2018). Language and culture revisited. Routledge.